I0466750

Vall-E2
Microsoft's Secret AI Speech Tool

The Hidden Powers, Ethical Dilemmas, and
Potential Impacts

Alejandro S. Diego

Copyright © Alejandro S. Diego, 2024.

All rights reserved. No part of this publication may be reproduced, distributed, or transmitted in any form or by any means, including photocopying, recording, or other electronic or mechanical methods, without the prior written permission of the publisher, except in the case of brief quotations embodied in critical reviews and certain other noncommercial uses permitted by copyright law.

Table of Contents

Introduction

In recent years, the realm of artificial intelligence has witnessed remarkable strides, particularly in the field of speech technology. The ability to create synthetic voices that closely mimic human speech has opened up a world of possibilities, transforming how we interact with machines and consume content. From virtual assistants to automated customer service, the applications of AI-driven speech tools are vast and continually expanding. Amidst these technological advancements, one project stands out, shrouded in both intrigue and potential: Microsoft's Vall-E2.

Imagine a tool so sophisticated that it can generate speech indistinguishable from a human voice. Vall-E2, Microsoft's latest innovation in neural codec language models, promises to revolutionize the text-to-speech landscape. Its capabilities extend beyond mere novelty; Vall-E2 represents a significant leap towards achieving human parity in synthetic speech. This means that the speech it generates is not only natural and fluent but also rich with the nuances of human intonation and emotion.

The implications of Vall-E2's development are profound. For the first time, a machine can produce speech that matches the intricacy and expressiveness of human communication. This breakthrough is not just a technical achievement; it heralds a new era in accessibility, content creation, and human-machine interaction. Virtual assistants equipped with Vall-E2 can offer more personalized and engaging experiences. Automated customer service systems can handle inquiries with a human-like warmth and understanding, enhancing user satisfaction. Content creators can now bring their words to life with voices that resonate authentically with their audiences.

Yet, the journey to this point has not been without challenges. Achieving such a high level of naturalness in synthetic speech required overcoming significant hurdles, particularly in managing repetitive patterns and ensuring coherence over long sequences. Microsoft's Vall-E2 addresses these issues with innovative solutions like repetition-aware sampling and group code modeling. These advancements ensure that the generated speech flows seamlessly, avoiding the pitfalls of robotic monotony and enhancing the overall quality and fluidity of the output.

As we delve into the world of Vall-E2, we will explore the intricacies of this groundbreaking technology, uncovering its hidden powers and the ethical dilemmas it presents. What makes Vall-E2 truly remarkable is not just its technical prowess but also the thoughtful approach Microsoft has taken in considering its broader impact. The decision to withhold Vall-E2 from public release, despite its astounding capabilities, underscores the company's commitment to responsible innovation. By keeping this technology under wraps, Microsoft acknowledges the potential risks of misuse, such as voice spoofing and impersonation, and emphasizes the importance of ethical considerations in the deployment of advanced AI.

In this book, we embark on a journey through the evolution of AI speech tools, tracing the development of Vall-E2 and its potential to reshape the future. We will delve into the technical marvels that make Vall-E2 a standout in the field, examine its real-world applications, and confront the ethical questions it raises. Through this exploration, you will gain a deeper understanding of how Vall-E2 represents not just a leap forward in technology but a pivotal moment in our relationship with artificial intelligence.

Prepare to be captivated by the story of Vall-E2, a tale of innovation, responsibility, and the tantalizing possibilities of a future where machines speak with the voice of humanity. As you turn the pages, let the wonder of this technological marvel and its implications unfold, sparking your imagination and curiosity about what lies ahead in the ever-evolving landscape of AI speech technology.

Chapter 1: The Evolution of AI Speech Tools

Artificial intelligence has long captured the imagination of researchers and the public alike, and one of its most fascinating branches is the development of AI speech tools. The journey from rudimentary text-to-speech systems to the sophisticated models we see today, like Microsoft's Vall-E2, is a testament to the relentless pursuit of innovation and the quest to make machines more human-like in their interactions.

The historical development of AI speech tools can be traced back to the mid-20th century. Early efforts in speech synthesis were rudimentary at best, producing robotic and unnatural sounds that bore little resemblance to human speech. One of the first significant milestones came in the 1960s with the creation of the IBM Shoebox, an early speech recognition system that could understand and respond to a limited vocabulary of spoken words.

This was a groundbreaking achievement, laying the foundation for future advancements.

The 1980s and 1990s saw substantial progress in the field, driven by the advent of digital signal processing. During this period, techniques such as formant synthesis, which mimicked the resonant frequencies of the human vocal tract, became prominent. These methods improved the naturalness of synthetic speech, although they still fell short of achieving true human-like fluency. It was also during this time that hidden Markov models (HMMs) were introduced, significantly enhancing speech recognition capabilities and paving the way for more sophisticated TTS systems.

The turn of the millennium marked a new era for AI speech technology with the emergence of concatenative synthesis. This approach, which involved piecing together snippets of recorded human speech, produced much more natural results than previous methods. Companies like AT&T and Microsoft began to develop commercial

TTS systems that could be used in various applications, from assistive technologies for the visually impaired to automated phone systems.

A major breakthrough occurred in the 2010s with the rise of deep learning. Neural networks, particularly recurrent neural networks (RNNs) and convolutional neural networks (CNNs), revolutionized the way speech synthesis and recognition were approached. Google's WaveNet, introduced in 2016, was a game-changer. WaveNet used deep generative models to produce remarkably realistic and natural-sounding speech, setting a new standard for the industry.

The introduction of transformers, a type of model architecture that handles sequential data more effectively, further propelled advancements in the field. Transformers enabled models to better understand context and maintain coherence over longer sequences, which is crucial for producing fluent and natural speech. OpenAI's GPT series and Google's BERT model are prime examples of how transformer-based architectures have been leveraged to improve AI language processing, including speech synthesis.

In this rapidly evolving landscape, Microsoft's Vall-E2 represents the latest pinnacle of achievement. Building on the foundation laid by its predecessors, Vall-E2 incorporates cutting-edge techniques such as repetition-aware sampling and group code modeling to address longstanding challenges in speech synthesis. These innovations ensure that the generated speech not only sounds natural but also maintains the rhythm and intonation of human speech, even over long and complex sentences.

The journey from the early days of synthetic speech to the sophisticated capabilities of Vall-E2 highlights the incredible progress made in the field of AI speech tools. Each milestone has brought us closer to creating machines that can communicate with us in ways that feel genuinely human. As we look to the future, the potential applications of these technologies are boundless, promising to transform industries and enhance our daily lives in ways we are only beginning to imagine.

Microsoft's journey in the realm of AI speech technology is a fascinating story of innovation, persistence, and transformative breakthroughs. From the early days of rudimentary speech systems to the cutting-edge advancements represented by Vall-E2, Microsoft's contributions have been pivotal in shaping the landscape of text-to-speech (TTS) and speech recognition technologies.

The journey began in the 1990s, when Microsoft first ventured into speech technology with the introduction of its Speech API (SAPI). This early framework allowed developers to integrate basic speech recognition and synthesis capabilities into their applications, marking Microsoft's initial foray into a field that would become increasingly important in the years to come. SAPI laid the groundwork for future developments and established Microsoft's commitment to advancing speech technology.

In the early 2000s, Microsoft made significant strides with the release of Microsoft Speech Server. This enterprise-grade product brought advanced speech recognition and synthesis capabilities to business applications, enabling more natural and efficient human-computer interactions. The Speech Server was instrumental in popularizing the use of speech technology in customer service and support applications, setting a standard for quality and reliability.

A major milestone came in 2010 with the launch of Microsoft's Tellme Networks, an acquisition that bolstered the company's expertise and resources in voice technology. Tellme Networks specialized in voice recognition and interactive voice response (IVR) systems, providing the technological backbone for Microsoft's expanding portfolio of speech-enabled applications. This acquisition signaled Microsoft's serious commitment to becoming a leader in the speech technology space.

The introduction of Cortana, Microsoft's digital assistant, in 2014 marked another significant advancement. Cortana leveraged sophisticated speech recognition and natural language processing (NLP) technologies to provide users with a highly interactive and personalized experience. This was a clear demonstration of how far Microsoft had come in developing intuitive and responsive speech technologies that could understand and act on complex voice commands.

Microsoft's commitment to AI speech technology was further solidified with the launch of Azure Cognitive Services in 2016. This suite of APIs offered developers access to a range of AI capabilities, including advanced speech recognition and synthesis. By making these tools widely available, Microsoft empowered a new wave of innovation, enabling developers to build applications that could understand and respond to human speech with unprecedented accuracy and naturalness.

The release of Custom Speech and Speech Studio in 2018 took this a step further, offering tailored speech recognition models that could be fine-tuned for specific vocabularies and acoustic environments. This customization capability was a game-changer for industries requiring specialized terminology and conditions, such as healthcare, finance, and telecommunications. It underscored Microsoft's commitment to providing versatile and adaptable speech solutions.

Microsoft's most recent and ambitious project, Vall-E2, represents the culmination of decades of research and development. Vall-E2 showcases the company's expertise in neural codec language models, pushing the boundaries of what is possible in text-to-speech synthesis. This model not only achieves human parity in terms of naturalness and fluency but also introduces groundbreaking innovations like repetition-aware sampling and group code modeling. These advancements address critical challenges in maintaining rhythm and coherence in generated speech, making Vall-E2 a truly revolutionary tool.

The evolution of Microsoft's AI speech technology is a testament to the company's relentless pursuit of excellence and innovation. From the early days of SAPI to the sophisticated capabilities of Vall-E2, Microsoft has consistently pushed the envelope, driving the field forward and setting new standards for what can be achieved. As we look to the future, it is clear that Microsoft will continue to be a major force in shaping the next generation of AI speech technologies, transforming how we interact with machines and enhancing the way we live and work.

Chapter 2: Unveiling Vall-E2

In the ever-evolving landscape of artificial intelligence, few innovations have sparked as much intrigue and excitement as Microsoft's Vall-E2. This cutting-edge text-to-speech (TTS) model represents a significant milestone in AI speech technology, pushing the boundaries of what machines can achieve in mimicking human speech. Vall-E2's development is not just a technical achievement; it is a beacon of the potential future where AI can communicate with us in ways that are almost indistinguishable from a human.

Vall-E2, the latest brainchild of Microsoft's AI research team, is an advanced neural codec language model specifically designed for zero-shot text-to-speech synthesis. This means that Vall-E2 can generate highly natural and fluent speech from text input without needing extensive prior training on specific voice samples. The significance of Vall-E2 lies in its ability to produce speech that matches the naturalness and expressiveness of human speech, a feat that has long been a holy grail in the field of AI.

The technology behind Vall-E2 is both sophisticated and innovative. At its core, Vall-E2 employs a neural codec model, which is a type of artificial neural network that processes and generates human-like speech. What sets Vall-E2 apart from its predecessors are its two groundbreaking enhancements: repetition-aware sampling and group code modeling.

Repetition-aware sampling addresses a common challenge in TTS systems—maintaining a natural rhythm and avoiding repetitive patterns in generated speech. Traditional models often struggle with creating long or complex sentences that sound fluid and natural, frequently falling into repetitive loops that detract from the overall quality. Vall-E2's repetition-aware sampling refines this process by focusing on detecting and managing repetitive elements during speech generation. This enhancement ensures that the output maintains a smooth and coherent flow, much like a human speaker would.

Group code modeling is another significant technological advancement in Vall-E2. This approach involves organizing similar linguistic or phonetic codes into specific groups, effectively managing and shortening the sequence length of the generated text. Handling long sequences can be computationally demanding and can degrade the performance of TTS models. By grouping related codes, Vall-E2 simplifies the processing of lengthy sequences, speeding up the inference process and enhancing the model's ability to handle complex speech tasks more efficiently. This grouping mechanism also helps Vall-E2 to better understand and generate the nuanced aspects of human speech, such as intonation and emotion, making the synthesized speech more diverse and contextually appropriate.

Microsoft's experiments with Vall-E2, conducted using the Liers speech and VCTK data sets, have demonstrated its superiority over previous zero-shot TTS systems. Vall-E2 excels in generating stable, consistent, and high-quality speech outputs, even when dealing with intricate sentence structures or repetitive phrases. The robustness of Vall-E2 ensures that the synthesized speech remains clear and intelligible across various contexts and use cases, a critical factor for its deployment in real-world applications.

The potential applications of Vall-E2 are vast and varied. In virtual assistants, Vall-E2 can offer a more personalized and engaging user experience, responding to queries with human-like warmth and naturalness. In customer service, it can enhance the quality of interactions, making automated responses more pleasant and effective. For content creators, Vall-E2 provides a powerful tool to bring written words to life, offering a range of voices that can match the intended tone and emotion of the content.

However, the significance of Vall-E2 extends beyond its technical capabilities. Microsoft's decision to keep Vall-E2 under wraps and not release it to the public underscores a responsible approach to technological innovation. The company recognizes the potential ethical dilemmas and risks associated with such powerful AI, including the possibility of voice spoofing and impersonation. By withholding Vall-E2 from commercial use, Microsoft aims to refine the technology further and develop safeguards to mitigate these risks, ensuring that when it is eventually released, it can be used responsibly and ethically.

Vall-E2 represents a monumental leap forward in AI speech technology. Its advanced neural codec model, combined with innovative techniques like repetition-aware sampling and group code modeling, enables it to generate speech that is astonishingly human-like. As we continue to explore the capabilities and implications of Vall-E2, it becomes clear that this technology has the potential to transform how we interact with machines, making our digital experiences more natural, engaging, and effective.

The allure of Vall-E2 lies in its remarkable ability to synthesize speech that mirrors the intricacies of human communication. This groundbreaking model, developed by Microsoft, embodies a series of advanced features that collectively elevate text-to-speech technology to new heights. Its key features and capabilities form the cornerstone of its unprecedented performance and versatility.

At the heart of Vall-E2 is its achievement of human parity in speech synthesis. This means that the speech generated by Vall-E2 is virtually indistinguishable from human speech in terms of naturalness and expressiveness. The model captures the subtleties of human intonation, rhythm, and emotion, creating a listening experience that feels authentically human. This breakthrough sets Vall-E2 apart from previous models, making it a significant leap forward in the realm of artificial intelligence.

One of the pivotal innovations within Vall-E2 is its repetition-aware sampling. Traditional TTS models often falter when faced with the challenge of maintaining a natural flow in lengthy or complex sentences, frequently producing repetitive and monotonous patterns. Vall-E2 addresses this issue by incorporating a sophisticated mechanism that detects and manages repetitive elements during the speech generation process. By refining the nucleus sampling method, Vall-E2 ensures that the output maintains a seamless and coherent flow, avoiding the pitfalls of robotic repetition. This enhancement markedly improves the quality and fluency of the synthesized speech, making it more engaging and lifelike.

Another standout feature of Vall-E2 is group code modeling. This approach involves organizing similar linguistic or phonetic codes into specific groups, which helps manage and shorten the sequence length of the generated text. Handling long sequences poses a significant challenge in TTS synthesis due to the increased computational load and potential for performance degradation. By grouping related codes, Vall-E2 simplifies the processing of lengthy sequences, accelerating the inference process and enhancing the model's efficiency. This technique not only improves the model's ability to generate nuanced aspects of human speech, such as intonation and emotion, but also ensures better performance across various linguistic contexts.

Vall-E2's robustness is evident in its ability to handle diverse and challenging speech scenarios with exceptional stability. Extensive experiments using data sets like Liers speech and VCTK have demonstrated Vall-E2's prowess in generating consistent, high-quality speech outputs even when confronted with intricate sentence structures or repetitive phrases. This robustness ensures that the synthesized speech remains clear and intelligible across different contexts and applications, a critical factor for real-world deployment.

One of the most impressive capabilities of Vall-E2 is its proficiency in zero-shot speech synthesis. This means Vall-E2 can generate high-quality speech using only a brief sample from an unseen speaker, capturing and reproducing unique vocal traits with remarkable accuracy. This ability is particularly valuable for applications that require personalized or consistent voice outputs, such as virtual assistants or automated narration services. Vall-E2's zero-shot synthesis ensures that the speech produced closely matches the original speaker's voice, enhancing the overall user experience and making interactions more personal and authentic.

Additionally, Vall-E2 excels in zero-shot speech continuation, a feature that allows the model to seamlessly continue speech from a brief initial audio sample while maintaining the speaker's characteristics and ensuring a smooth transition.

With just a three-second prefix as the speaker prompt, Vall-E2 can extend the speech naturally, demonstrating its advanced understanding and replication of a speaker's unique voice attributes from minimal input.

Flexibility is another hallmark of Vall-E2. The model can synthesize speech from various lengths of speaker prompts, whether using a three-second, five-second, or ten-second sample. This adaptability is crucial for meeting different contextual needs and requirements, providing users with the ability to generate high-quality speech from varying amounts of input data. This capability ensures that Vall-E2 can be tailored to the specific needs of different applications, making it a versatile tool for developers and content creators.

Despite its advanced capabilities, Microsoft has chosen to withhold Vall-E2 from public release due to potential ethical and security concerns. The model's ability to mimic human voices so convincingly raises risks related to voice spoofing and impersonation, which could be exploited for deceptive practices. By keeping Vall-E2 under wraps, Microsoft underscores its commitment to responsible innovation, emphasizing the importance of refining the technology and developing safeguards before considering broader access.

The potential applications of Vall-E2 are vast and varied. In virtual assistants, Vall-E2 can provide more personalized and engaging user experiences, responding with human-like warmth and naturalness. Automated customer service systems can benefit from Vall-E2's ability to handle inquiries with clarity and responsiveness, improving user satisfaction. Content creators can leverage Vall-E2 to bring their written words to life, offering a range of voices that match the intended tone and emotion of their content. As we explore the potential applications and ethical implications of Vall-E2, it is clear that this technology has the potential to transform how we interact with machines, making our digital experiences more natural, engaging, and effective.

Chapter 3: Technical Innovations in Vall-E2

One of the most transformative features of Vall-E2 is its innovative approach to repetition-aware sampling. This advancement is crucial in overcoming a common challenge faced by traditional text-to-speech (TTS) models: maintaining a natural rhythm and avoiding repetitive patterns. Understanding the intricacies of this feature reveals how Vall-E2 sets a new standard in speech synthesis.

Repetition-aware sampling fundamentally changes how Vall-E2 handles the generation of speech. In traditional TTS models, generating long or complex sentences often results in speech that sounds robotic or monotonous due to repetitive sequences of tokens. These repetitive patterns break the natural flow of speech, making it less engaging and more difficult to listen to. Vall-E2 addresses this issue head-on by incorporating a sophisticated mechanism designed to detect and manage these repetitive elements during the speech generation process.

The importance of maintaining a natural rhythm in speech cannot be overstated. Human speech is characterized by its variability and fluidity, with natural pauses, emphasis, and intonation that convey meaning and emotion. When a TTS model fails to replicate these characteristics, the resulting speech can feel artificial and unconvincing. By focusing on repetition-aware sampling, Vall-E2 ensures that the speech it generates mirrors the dynamic nature of human conversation, making it more relatable and pleasant to listen to.

At the core of repetition-aware sampling is the refinement of the nucleus sampling process. Nucleus sampling is a method used in natural language processing to generate text by selecting tokens based on their probabilities. In traditional models, this method can sometimes produce repetitive sequences, which disrupt the naturalness of the generated speech. Vall-E2 enhances this process by taking token repetition into account during decoding.

This enhancement works by analyzing the generated tokens for potential repetitions and adjusting the selection process accordingly. When Vall-E2 detects a sequence of tokens that might lead to repetition, it modifies the sampling probabilities to favor more diverse and contextually appropriate tokens. This adjustment prevents the model from getting stuck in repetitive loops and ensures a more varied and natural output.

The impact of this refinement on the overall quality and fluency of the synthesized speech is significant. By effectively managing repetition, Vall-E2 produces speech that flows more smoothly, with natural intonation and rhythm. This makes the generated speech sound more human-like, enhancing its usability in various applications, from virtual assistants to automated customer service.

In practical terms, repetition-aware sampling allows Vall-E2 to handle a wider range of speech scenarios with ease. Whether generating long, complex sentences or simple, direct responses, Vall-E2 can maintain a consistent level of quality and naturalness. This robustness is crucial for real-world applications where the model needs to adapt to different contexts and user needs without compromising on the quality of the output.

The benefits of repetition-aware sampling extend beyond just avoiding monotony. It also enhances the coherence of the synthesized speech. By ensuring that the generated tokens are contextually appropriate and diverse, Vall-E2 maintains a logical flow in its speech, making it easier for listeners to follow and understand. This is particularly important in applications where clarity and intelligibility are paramount, such as in educational tools or accessibility services.

In conclusion, repetition-aware sampling is a key feature that sets Vall-E2 apart from traditional TTS models. By refining the nucleus sampling process and effectively managing repetitive elements, Vall-E2 ensures that the speech it generates maintains a natural rhythm and fluidity. This advancement not only enhances the quality and naturalness of the synthesized speech but also broadens its applicability across various domains. As we continue to explore the capabilities of Vall-E2, the importance of such innovations becomes increasingly clear, highlighting the potential of AI to transform our interactions with technology in profound and meaningful ways.

Group code modeling is another pivotal innovation within Vall-E2, contributing significantly to its advanced capabilities in text-to-speech synthesis. This approach involves organizing similar linguistic or phonetic codes into specific groups, which simplifies the processing of lengthy sequences and enhances both the naturalness and performance of the generated speech.

In traditional text-to-speech models, handling long sequences of text poses a significant challenge. As the length of the sequence increases, so does the computational load required to process it. This often leads to performance degradation and a reduction in the quality of the synthesized speech. Long sequences can become cumbersome, resulting in speech that lacks coherence and naturalness. Vall-E2 tackles this issue with its group code modeling technique, which streamlines the processing of these lengthy sequences.

The fundamental idea behind group code modeling is to categorize related linguistic or phonetic codes into groups. By doing so, Vall-E2 can manage these grouped codes more efficiently than if each code were processed individually. This grouping reduces the complexity of the sequence, making it easier and faster for the model to generate speech. The result is a significant improvement in the model's efficiency, allowing it to handle longer sequences without sacrificing performance.

This simplification of processing is crucial for several reasons. Firstly, it reduces the computational resources required to generate speech, enabling faster and more responsive performance. This is particularly important in real-time applications, such as virtual assistants and live customer service interactions, where delays can negatively impact the user experience. Secondly, it allows Vall-E2 to maintain a high level of quality and naturalness in the synthesized speech, even when dealing with complex or extended text inputs.

The enhancement of naturalness in speech synthesis through group code modeling is another major benefit. Human speech is characterized by its fluidity and variation in intonation, rhythm, and emphasis. Traditional models often struggle to replicate these nuances, especially when processing long sequences. By grouping related codes, Vall-E2 can better understand and generate these subtle variations in speech, resulting in a more natural and human-like output.

Group code modeling also contributes to the model's ability to generate speech that is contextually appropriate and diverse. By managing the sequence length more effectively, Vall-E2 can focus on producing speech that aligns closely with the intended meaning and emotion of the text. This leads to more engaging and authentic interactions, enhancing the overall user experience.

In practical terms, the benefits of group code modeling extend to a wide range of applications. In virtual assistants, for example, the ability to generate natural and coherent responses to complex queries is crucial. Users expect interactions that feel fluid and responsive, without the stilted or repetitive patterns that can break the immersion. Vall-E2's group code modeling ensures that these interactions are as close to human conversation as possible, improving user satisfaction and engagement.

Similarly, in automated customer service systems, the ability to handle long and detailed inquiries with clarity and naturalness can significantly enhance the quality of service. Customers are more likely to have positive experiences when their interactions feel personal and understanding, which Vall-E2 can provide through its advanced speech synthesis capabilities.

Content creation is another area where group code modeling shines. Whether generating voiceovers for videos, podcasts, or audiobooks, Vall-E2's ability to produce natural-sounding speech over extended periods is invaluable. Content creators can rely on Vall-E2 to deliver consistent and high-quality narration that matches the tone and emotion of their scripts, making their work more impactful and engaging.

In conclusion, group code modeling is a key feature that contributes to the exceptional performance of Vall-E2. By simplifying the processing of lengthy sequences and enhancing the naturalness of the generated speech, this technique ensures that Vall-E2 can deliver high-quality, human-like speech across a variety of applications. As we continue to explore the capabilities of Vall-E2, the significance of group code modeling becomes increasingly evident, highlighting its role in advancing the field of text-to-speech technology and transforming our interactions with AI.

Chapter 4: Performance and Capabilities

The true test of any advanced AI model lies in its performance across diverse and challenging scenarios. Microsoft's Vall-E2 has been rigorously tested using the Liers speech and VCTK data sets, which are well-respected benchmarks in the field of speech synthesis. These experiments have showcased Vall-E2's exceptional capabilities and highlighted its achievements in maintaining high-quality speech synthesis under various conditions.

The Liers speech and VCTK data sets provide a comprehensive range of speech samples that include different accents, dialects, and speaking styles. This diversity is crucial for evaluating the robustness and flexibility of Vall-E2. By training and testing the model on such varied data, Microsoft ensured that Vall-E2 could handle real-world applications where speech input is rarely uniform and often complex.

One of the most significant findings from these experiments is Vall-E2's robustness in handling diverse and challenging speech scenarios. Traditional text-to-speech models often struggle with maintaining quality when faced with complex sentence structures or atypical speech patterns. Vall-E2, however, excels in generating stable and consistent speech outputs even under these conditions. This robustness is a testament to the model's sophisticated architecture and advanced features like repetition-aware sampling and group code modeling.

In practical terms, this means that Vall-E2 can produce high-quality speech regardless of the complexity of the input. Whether the text involves long, intricate sentences with multiple clauses or short, sharp statements, Vall-E2 maintains a natural rhythm and fluidity. This capability is particularly valuable in applications that require adaptability and precision, such as virtual assistants, customer service bots, and content creation tools.

The experiments also highlighted Vall-E2's ability to maintain high-quality speech synthesis across different linguistic contexts. The Liers speech and VCTK data sets include a variety of accents and dialects, which pose a significant challenge for TTS models. Vall-E2 demonstrated its proficiency in generating speech that not only sounds natural but also accurately reflects the nuances of different accents and speaking styles. This feature is crucial for creating inclusive and accessible AI systems that can cater to a global audience.

Moreover, Vall-E2's achievements in maintaining high-quality speech synthesis are evident in its ability to handle repetitive and complex phrases without losing coherence. Traditional models often fall into patterns of unnatural repetition, especially when dealing with extended text. Vall-E2's repetition-aware sampling technique effectively mitigates this issue, ensuring that the generated speech remains engaging and lifelike. This advancement significantly enhances the listening experience, making Vall-E2 a more practical and effective tool for various applications.

The experimental results also underscore Vall-E2's capability in zero-shot speech synthesis, where the model generates speech using only a brief sample from an unseen speaker. This feature is particularly impressive, as it demonstrates Vall-E2's ability to capture and replicate unique vocal traits with minimal input. The model's performance in zero-shot scenarios highlights its potential for personalized voice applications, where users can quickly create custom voices that sound remarkably close to their own or any desired speaker.

Another noteworthy achievement of Vall-E2 is its proficiency in zero-shot speech continuation. In the experiments, Vall-E2 was able to seamlessly continue speech from a brief initial audio sample while maintaining the speaker's characteristics and ensuring a smooth transition. This ability to extend speech naturally from a short prompt showcases Vall-E2's deep understanding of vocal attributes and context, making it an invaluable tool for applications requiring extended dialogue or narration.

The flexibility of Vall-E2 in synthesizing speech from various lengths of speaker prompts further demonstrates its adaptability. Whether using a three-second, five-second, or ten-second sample, Vall-E2 consistently produced accurate and natural-sounding speech. This flexibility is crucial for adapting to different contexts and requirements, providing users with the ability to generate high-quality speech from varying amounts of input data.

In conclusion, the results from experiments using the Liers speech and VCTK data sets highlight Vall-E2's exceptional capabilities in handling diverse and challenging speech scenarios. The model's robustness, adaptability, and high-quality speech synthesis set a new standard in the field of text-to-speech technology. Vall-E2's advanced features, such as repetition-aware sampling and group code modeling, ensure that it can produce natural, engaging, and contextually appropriate speech across a wide range of applications. These achievements underscore Vall-E2's potential to transform our interactions with AI, making digital experiences more immersive and human-like.

Chapter 5: Real-World Applications

The versatility and advanced capabilities of Vall-E2 open up a multitude of real-world applications, each benefiting significantly from the model's ability to generate natural, human-like speech. These applications span various domains, including virtual assistants, customer service, content creation, accessibility, and entertainment, highlighting Vall-E2's potential to transform our interactions with technology and enhance user experiences across the board.

One of the most promising applications of Vall-E2 is in virtual assistants. Virtual assistants like Cortana, Alexa, and Siri have become integral parts of our daily lives, assisting with tasks ranging from setting reminders to providing weather updates. Vall-E2's ability to produce speech that matches human naturalness and expressiveness elevates these interactions to a new level. Users can enjoy more engaging and responsive conversations with their virtual assistants, which can now respond with warmth, emotion, and nuanced intonation. This improvement not only enhances user satisfaction but also makes virtual assistants more effective in understanding and responding to complex queries.

In the realm of customer service, Vall-E2 offers significant benefits by enabling automated systems to handle inquiries with a level of clarity and empathy previously unattainable with traditional TTS models. Customer service bots powered by Vall-E2 can manage a wide range of tasks, from answering frequently asked questions to resolving issues, all while maintaining a natural and conversational tone. This naturalness helps in building trust and rapport with customers, improving their overall experience. Additionally, the model's robustness in handling diverse and challenging speech scenarios ensures that it can effectively manage various accents and dialects, making it a versatile tool for global customer service operations.

Content creation is another area where Vall-E2's capabilities shine. Content creators, whether they are producing podcasts, audiobooks, videos, or educational materials, can leverage Vall-E2 to generate high-quality voiceovers that align perfectly with their scripts. The model's proficiency in capturing nuances of human speech, including intonation and emotion, allows creators to produce engaging and immersive audio content. Vall-E2 can also streamline the production process by generating voiceovers quickly and efficiently, reducing the time and cost associated with traditional voice recording methods.

Vall-E2's potential to improve accessibility for individuals with speech impairments is particularly noteworthy. For people who have difficulty speaking, whether due to medical conditions or disabilities, Vall-E2 can provide personalized and natural-sounding voice assistance. By generating speech that closely matches the user's desired vocal characteristics, Vall-E2 can help individuals communicate more effectively, both in personal and professional settings. This application not only enhances the quality of life for individuals with speech impairments but also promotes greater inclusivity and participation in various aspects of society.

The entertainment industry stands to benefit immensely from Vall-E2's advanced speech synthesis capabilities. One exciting application is in the creation of unique voiceovers for characters in movies, video games, and animations. Vall-E2 can generate a diverse range of voices, each with its own distinct personality and emotional depth. This capability allows for the creation of more dynamic and engaging characters, enhancing the storytelling experience for audiences. Moreover, the ability to produce high-quality voiceovers quickly and efficiently can significantly reduce production times and costs, making it easier for creators to bring their visions to life.

Another area within entertainment where Vall-E2 can make a substantial impact is in the realm of personalized content. For instance, interactive stories and games can leverage Vall-E2 to provide customized voice responses based on user choices, creating a more immersive and engaging experience. This level of interactivity and personalization can enhance user engagement and make entertainment experiences more enjoyable and memorable.

In conclusion, Vall-E2's advanced features and capabilities make it an invaluable tool across a wide range of real-world applications. From enhancing virtual assistants and customer service interactions to empowering content creators and improving accessibility for individuals with speech impairments, Vall-E2 has the potential to transform how we interact with technology. Additionally, its ability to generate unique and expressive voiceovers opens up new possibilities in the entertainment industry, offering more dynamic and immersive experiences for audiences. As we continue to explore and develop these applications, Vall-E2 stands as a testament to the transformative power of AI in creating more natural, engaging, and inclusive digital experiences.

Chapter 6: Ethical Considerations and Challenges

As we continue to advance in the realm of artificial intelligence, the ethical implications of these innovations become increasingly significant. The development of sophisticated AI speech tools like Vall-E2 brings about numerous benefits, but it also raises important ethical questions that must be addressed to ensure responsible and safe use. The capabilities of Vall-E2, while impressive, come with potential risks, particularly concerning voice spoofing and impersonation.

Voice spoofing and impersonation are serious concerns in the age of advanced AI speech tools. Vall-E2's ability to generate speech that is virtually indistinguishable from human voices means that, in the wrong hands, this technology could be used for malicious purposes. For example, individuals could use Vall-E2 to create convincing audio clips that impersonate someone's voice, potentially leading to identity theft, fraud, or other forms of deception.

The potential for such misuse highlights the need for stringent ethical guidelines and safeguards.

Recognizing these risks, Microsoft has taken a cautious and responsible approach by deciding to keep Vall-E2 under wraps for the time being. This decision reflects the company's commitment to ethical considerations and the potential societal impact of releasing such powerful technology. By withholding Vall-E2 from public and commercial use, Microsoft aims to prevent the technology from being exploited for harmful purposes while further refining its capabilities and developing necessary safeguards.

Microsoft's decision is a prudent step in ensuring that the deployment of Vall-E2 is conducted responsibly. The company is focusing on understanding the full extent of Vall-E2's potential applications and implications in controlled environments. This approach allows Microsoft to study the model's behavior, identify potential vulnerabilities, and develop strategies to mitigate risks before considering a broader release.

To responsibly refine and safeguard Vall-E2, Microsoft is likely to implement several measures. These may include developing robust security protocols to detect and prevent misuse, such as voice authentication mechanisms that can distinguish between genuine and AI-generated speech. Additionally, Microsoft could establish clear guidelines and ethical standards for the use of Vall-E2, ensuring that the technology is applied in ways that benefit society and minimize harm.

Transparency and accountability are also crucial in the responsible development of AI technologies. By openly discussing the ethical implications and potential risks associated with Vall-E2, Microsoft sets a precedent for other companies and researchers in the field. This transparency fosters a collaborative environment where stakeholders can work together to address ethical concerns and develop best practices for AI speech tools.

Furthermore, Microsoft's commitment to ethical AI extends to its broader initiatives, such as the AI for Good program, which aims to leverage AI technology to address global challenges and improve lives. By aligning Vall-E2 with these ethical principles, Microsoft ensures that its advancements in AI speech technology contribute positively to society.

The ethical implications of advanced AI speech tools like Vall-E2 are multifaceted and require careful consideration. While the technology offers tremendous potential for improving communication, accessibility, and entertainment, it also poses significant risks if misused. Microsoft's decision to keep Vall-E2 under wraps and focus on refining and safeguarding the technology demonstrates a responsible approach to AI development. By prioritizing ethical considerations and transparency, Microsoft is setting a standard for the industry, ensuring that the benefits of AI speech technology are realized while minimizing potential harm.

As we continue to explore the possibilities of AI speech tools, it is imperative that we remain vigilant about their ethical implications. The balance between innovation and responsibility will determine how these technologies shape our future. With careful stewardship and a commitment to ethical principles, we can harness the power of AI speech tools like Vall-E2 to create a more inclusive, engaging, and secure digital landscape.

Chapter 7: Future Prospects of AI Speech Technology

The rapid advancement of AI speech technology, exemplified by Vall-E2, invites exciting speculation about the future. As we look ahead, it is clear that the development of even more sophisticated and capable AI speech models will continue to transform various industries, bringing about profound changes in how we interact with technology and each other. Vall-E2 is just the beginning of a new era in speech synthesis, and the potential advancements on the horizon promise to push the boundaries of what is possible.

Future advancements in AI speech technology are likely to focus on further enhancing the naturalness and expressiveness of synthesized speech. One area of development could be the integration of more complex emotional and contextual understanding into speech models. This would enable AI to generate speech that not only sounds human but also responds to the emotional tone and context of the conversation, creating more empathetic and engaging interactions. For instance, virtual assistants could provide comfort and support in sensitive situations or deliver enthusiastic responses in exciting contexts, making interactions feel more personal and authentic.

Another anticipated advancement is the improvement of multilingual capabilities. Current models like Vall-E2 already handle multiple languages, but future iterations could seamlessly switch between languages and dialects within a single conversation, catering to the needs of global users. This would be particularly beneficial in customer service and educational applications, where the ability to understand and respond in multiple languages can significantly enhance user experience and accessibility.

The potential impacts of these advancements on various industries are vast. In healthcare, for example, more advanced AI speech tools could be used to provide better support for patients through virtual health assistants that can offer personalized advice, reminders, and even emotional support. This could improve patient outcomes by ensuring that individuals adhere to treatment plans and receive timely interventions.

In the field of education, AI speech models could revolutionize language learning and accessibility. Students could engage with virtual tutors that provide real-time feedback and support, making learning more interactive and effective. Additionally, AI speech technology could make educational content more accessible to students with disabilities, providing tailored support that meets their individual needs.

The entertainment industry stands to benefit immensely from future advancements in AI speech technology. More sophisticated voice synthesis could lead to the creation of dynamic and interactive media experiences, such as personalized storylines in video games where characters respond uniquely to each player's actions and choices. This level of interactivity could also extend to immersive virtual reality environments, where AI-generated characters provide more realistic and engaging interactions.

As for Vall-E2, ongoing research and future plans are likely focused on addressing the ethical considerations and refining its capabilities. Microsoft's decision to keep Vall-E2 under wraps indicates a commitment to responsible innovation, suggesting that the company will continue to explore ways to mitigate potential risks associated with the technology. This might involve developing robust mechanisms for verifying the authenticity of AI-generated speech to prevent misuse such as voice spoofing and impersonation.

In addition to refining ethical safeguards, future plans for Vall-E2 may include expanding its applications and integrating it more deeply into Microsoft's ecosystem of products and services. For instance, Vall-E2 could be incorporated into Microsoft Teams to enhance virtual meetings with more natural and expressive speech synthesis, or integrated into Microsoft Azure to provide advanced TTS capabilities for developers building their own applications.

Furthermore, collaboration with researchers and other industry stakeholders will likely play a key role in the ongoing development of Vall-E2. By sharing insights and advancements, Microsoft can contribute to the broader goal of creating AI technologies that are not only powerful and versatile but also ethical and beneficial to society.

In conclusion, the future of AI speech technology is incredibly promising, with advancements set to further enhance the naturalness, expressiveness, and versatility of synthesized speech. These developments will have far-reaching impacts across various industries, improving healthcare, education, entertainment, and more. Ongoing research and future plans for Vall-E2 will focus on refining its capabilities and ensuring ethical use, paving the way for a future where AI speech technology enriches our lives in meaningful and responsible ways. As we continue to push the boundaries of what AI can achieve, the potential for creating more natural, engaging, and inclusive digital experiences is boundless.

Conclusion

The journey through the development and implications of Vall-E2 has highlighted the extraordinary advancements in AI speech technology. From its groundbreaking features like repetition-aware sampling and group code modeling to its impressive performance in handling diverse and challenging speech scenarios, Vall-E2 stands at the forefront of text-to-speech synthesis. This model not only achieves human parity in generating natural and expressive speech but also sets a new standard for the industry.

Vall-E2's potential applications are vast, spanning virtual assistants, customer service, content creation, accessibility for individuals with speech impairments, and the entertainment industry. Each application area benefits significantly from Vall-E2's ability to produce high-quality, human-like speech, enhancing user experience and engagement. Whether providing more natural interactions with virtual assistants or enabling personalized and realistic voiceovers in entertainment, Vall-E2 demonstrates the transformative power of advanced AI speech technology.

However, with these advancements come significant ethical considerations. The potential for misuse, such as voice spoofing and impersonation, underscores the importance of responsible development and deployment. Microsoft's decision to keep Vall-E2 under wraps, focusing on further refinement and the development of safeguards, exemplifies a commitment to ethical innovation. This responsible approach ensures that the technology can be utilized for the benefit of society while minimizing potential harm.

Balancing technological advancements with ethical responsibility is crucial as we move forward. It involves not only addressing the immediate risks but also anticipating future challenges and opportunities. Transparency, accountability, and collaboration among stakeholders are essential to navigating these complexities and ensuring that AI speech technology is developed and used in ways that align with societal values and norms.

Looking to the future, the potential of AI speech technology is boundless. We can expect further enhancements in naturalness and expressiveness, better emotional and contextual understanding, and improved multilingual capabilities. These advancements will continue to transform industries, from healthcare and education to entertainment and beyond, creating more immersive, accessible, and personalized experiences.

In conclusion, Vall-E2 represents a monumental leap forward in AI speech technology. Its advanced features and capabilities have the potential to revolutionize how we interact with machines, making digital experiences more natural and engaging. However, the path forward must be tread with care, balancing innovation with ethical responsibility. By fostering a culture of responsible

AI development, we can harness the power of technologies like Vall-E2 to create a future where AI enhances our lives in profound and positive ways. As we continue to explore and develop these technologies, the possibilities for creating more inclusive, dynamic, and human-like digital interactions are truly limitless.

www.ingramcontent.com/pod-product-compliance
Lightning Source LLC
Chambersburg PA
CBHW071957210526
45479CB00003B/972